Ripley's
WHALES AND DOLPHINS
Believe It or Not!®

Ripley
PUBLISHING
Aberdeenshire

3149560

D1646983

Written by Camilla de la Bedoyere
Consultants Barbara Taylor, Joe Choromanski

PUBLISHING

Publisher Anne Marshall

Editorial Director Rebecca Miles
Project Editor Charlotte Howell
Picture Researchers Michelle Foster, Charlotte Howell
Proofreader Lisa Regan
Indexer Hilary Bird

Art Director Sam South
Senior Designer Michelle Foster
Design Dynamo Design
Reprographics Juice Creative Ltd

www.ripleybooks.com

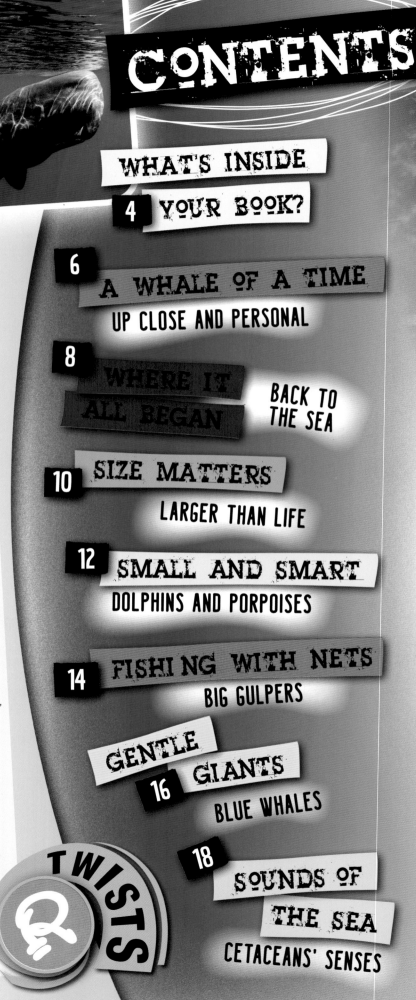

PAGE 33

CONTENTS

TWISTS

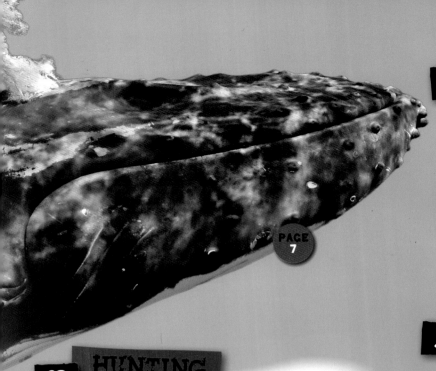

PAGE 7

PAGE 12

GIANTS OF THE SEA

BRILLIANT BEASTS

Orcas – also known as killer whales – come from fearsome families. A mother orca and her children prowl through the ocean, seeking other animals to hunt and eat. They are fast, agile, intelligent predators – and full of surprises.

WHAT'S INSIDE YOUR BOOK?

Orcas are a type of toothed whale – with up to 52 teeth!

They can grow to 9 m long.

Orcas can be found in all of the oceans in the world.

Our planet's deep blue oceans are home to an extraordinary group of animals. Whales and dolphins roam through the seas on incredible journeys to explore new places, meet up with old friends and forge new families.

If you think that whales and dolphins are closely related to fish, you'd be wrong. It's hard to believe, but they have more in common with hippos and humans than they do with sharks or salmon. There are lots more amazing things to discover about these magnificent, massive and majestic beasts.

TWISTS

Ripley explains...
See the 'Ripley explains' panels for extra info from our whale and dolphin experts.

Read more unbelievable facts when you spot a Key Facts box.

Look out for the 'Twist It' column on some pages. Twist the book to find out more amazing facts about whales and dolphins.

These books are about 'Believe It or Not!' – amazing facts, feats and things that make you go 'Wow!'

ALL AND SMART

S AND PORPOISES

d porpoises are small toothed
y look pretty similar, but dolphins
eak-shaped mouths.

phins have a reputation as kind,
als, they are ruthless predators of the
or killer whales, are members of this
they are some of the planet's most
d savage hunters.

TWIST IT!

IN A SPIN

Spinner dolphins love to leap out of the water and spin around and around before splashing back into the sea. Some can spin seven times in a single leap. No one really knows why they do this, but it may help them to get rid of little bugs that burrow into their skin, or it may be to do with communication or play.

KEY FACTS

- Dolphins have a lump of fatty tissue under the skin of the forehead called a melon.
- Dolphins have lots of cone-shaped teeth in their mouth.
- A dolphin does not have ears on the outside of its head. It only has inner ears, which take sound and turn it into messages for the brain.

Ripley's Believe It or Not!
This dolphin takes a leap over an unsuspecting surfer in Australia! Photographer Matt Hutton caught the rare sight on camera when he decided to try out surf-photography.

Dolphins have been badly affected by pollution in the oceans and seas. Poisons, especially the deadly metal mercury, are found in the fish they eat, and are then stored in their body.

Dolphins cannot smell. They lost that sense during evolution, when their nostrils moved to the top of their head and became their blowhole.

The shortest dolphins measure less than 150 cm long.

A harbour porpoise has between 86 and 106 teeth. It uses them to grip onto slippery fish.

Dall's porpoises are the most hunted of all cetaceans in the world. Human hunters have killed more than half a million of them for food in the last 50 years.

SMALL STATS

When a dolphin mother swims at top speed her little calf can keep up, but how? The baby swims in its mother's slipstream, a hair's breadth away from her. The slipstream is the area of water close to her body where there is less drag, making it easier for the baby to keep up with her.

The slipstream is created by the mother's body as it moves through the water – helping the baby to swim by her side.

HARBOUR PORPOIS

There are six species of porpo
and one of the smallest is the hart
porpoise. Porpoises usually live in gro
of 12 and they hunt fish together, o
shellfish found on the seabed. Har
porpoises live mostly in the
but have been spotted in ri

Porpoises have a round head and face. They do not have a dolphin's long 'beak'. Porpoises have spade-like teeth.

On the move

hins and porpoises are fast swimmers, and some can reach top
more than 55 km/h. Moving quickly takes a lot of energy – and
so these cetaceans often leap out of the water to breathe as
swimming. As they 'fly' through the air, the animals can stay
of the jaws of any chasing predators, while getting enough
air to help power their getaway.

BIG WORD ALERT
PREDATOR
An animal that hunts other animals to eat.

Found a new word? Big Word Alert will explain it for you.

Whales sleep by switching off one half of their brain at a time!

When whales spout water from their blowhole they breathe out – and most of them have stinky breath!

Bowhead whales may live to 200 years of age – or more!

Many whales listen using their jawbones!

One species of whale grows a single tooth up to 3 m long.

Dolphins can learn to understand and follow simple instructions.

Some whales are nearly blind but can still find their way around underwater.

Turn over to find out more about whales and dolphins.

A WHALE OF A TIME

UP CLOSE AND PERSONAL

If you want to get to know a whale a little better you need to get close, and really check it out. It's a bit tricky to do that when a whale is underwater, so we've done some research for you.

Whales and dolphins belong to a family of animals called cetaceans (say: set-ay-shuns). They are mammals – which means that, like humans, horses and hippos, they have hair and feed their babies with milk. Most mammals live on land, but cetaceans are perfectly adapted for a life in the world's oceans.

Ripley explains... Whale, human, fish

Whales and fish may look quite similar, and even lead fairly similar lives – but they belong to very different groups of animals: whales are mammals, like humans.

	Whale	Human	Fish
Lives in the sea	✓	✗	✓
Has limbs e.g. legs/flippers	✓	✓	✗
Breathes air	✓	✓	✗
Big brain	✓	✓	✗
Feeds young with milk	✓	✓	✗
Has a good body shape for swimming	✓	✗	✓

Invisible legs

Cetaceans may look as if they don't have any limbs (such as legs, arms or wings), but look again, and you will see them.

Shoulder blade.

The back legs are no longer used. Over millions of years they have mostly disappeared.

Tiny bones are all that's left of the back legs and pelvis.

Both front legs have become flippers, which are used for turning left or right when swimming.

Whales and dolphins are fighting to survive in our modern world. At least nine species of whales are in real danger of dying out completely.

Cetaceans don't need to drink water because they can get all the water they need from the food they eat.

Female cetaceans are called cows, the males are called bulls, and the babies are called calves.

Not all adult whales have hair on their heads, but they all sprouted some hair when they were babies developing inside their mother's body.

UNDERWATER LIFE

Make no bones about it

Cetaceans' dorsal fins don't have bones inside them – unlike the fins on a fish's back. That's why they sometimes droop, especially in orcas, which have the largest dorsal fins – reaching up to 2 m high. A blue whale's dorsal fin is just 40 cm in height, and some whales, such as belugas, don't have a dorsal fin at all.

Invisible waste gases are forced out of a whale's blowhole, with the water or water vapour, when they breathe out.

Coming up for air

Whales and dolphins cannot breathe underwater. They need to come to the water's surface to breathe air. Their nostrils are on the top of their head, and are called blowholes. Some whales have one blowhole, and some have two.

WHERE IT ALL BEGAN

BACK TO THE SEA

Long ago, the ancestors of whales lived on land. Then they discovered that there was plenty of food in the oceans – and few predators.

So, about 50 million years ago these creatures began a life in the water where their bodies changed and adapted to the new habitat. Now, take a deep breath and discover how whales became the mammal masters of the ocean.

Big change

Ancient whale relatives that lived on land breathed air through their mouth and nostrils, just like us. Most animals that live in the sea can take oxygen from the water, but whales and dolphins still get their oxygen from the air. During evolution, their nostrils moved to the top of their head, creating the blowhole. They breathe air through the blowhole at the surface.

Pakicetus skeleton →

Ambulocetus skeleton →

Going back in time

Look closely at a whale's body, and its ways of life, and you will see the secrets of its land-living past.

* Breathes air
* Has hair (not very much though!)
* Feeds its young with milk
* Has a skeleton that gives clues to how it evolved from a land-living animal

Pakicetus

The earliest whale ancestors were called *Pakicetus*. These were furry wolf-like animals that lived by the sea. They did not look much like whales, but their skulls were similar.

When: about 50 million years ago
Length: 1.7 metres

Ambulocetus

Early whales called *Ambulocetus* began to have similarites to today's whales and they lived in water. They had short legs and their hands and feet were shaped like paddles. Their tail was big and powerful.

When: about 48 million years ago
Length: 4 metres

Dorudon

Dorudon is a another early whale. It probably swam like a dolphin and hunted fish. The pelvic (hip) bones had almost completely disappeared (see left) along with the back legs.

When: 40-36 million years ago

Length: 4.4 metres

Breathe deep

Whales stay underwater for a long time because they have evolved to be able to hold their breath for a long time. They don't have particularly big lungs, but they are able to use almost every scrap of oxygen they take in. They can also fill their lungs in just two seconds, and take in about 3,000 times as much air as we do when we inhale (breathe in).

Atlantic spotted dolphin

Turn over to find out more about toothed and baleen whales...

Atlantic spotted dolphin skeleton

Toothed whales

Around 30 million years ago, two types of cetacean (marine mammals) had evolved to become today's modern whales and dolphins.

Whoa—the largest mouth of any animal!

Super spray

When whales breathe out they often make a spout of water or mist, which can be seen from far away, and is quite noisy! When a whale swims, muscles close the blowhole so water doesn't get in.

Dorudon skeleton

Pelvic bones

BIG WORD ALERT

EVOLUTION

The way an animal changes over time.

Baleen whales

Bowhead whale

Bowhead whale skeleton

Pelvic bones

SIZE MATTERS

LARGER THAN LIFE

Whales grow bigger than any other animal we know about – even bigger than dinosaurs.

The oceans are dense – that means they can support the weight of heavy things, making it easier for big animals to survive. Big animals need lots of food, but they can travel far and fast to find it. There are 85 species (types) of whales, dolphins and porpoises, but they can be split into just two groups: the **toothed whales** and the **baleen whales.**

Bottlenose dolphin

TOOTHED WHALES

- All dolphins are toothed whales.
- Toothed whales are also called Odontoceti.
- There are 71 species.
- They hunt their prey using echolocation.
- Most are small to medium sized.
- Males are usually bigger than females.
- They have one blowhole.

Vaquita 1.5 m

Dall's porpoise 2 m

Bottlenose dolphin 4 m

Sperm whale 20 m

Beluga 6 m

Short-finned pilot whale 8 m

Orca (killer whale) 9 m

Male orcas (killer whales) have a huge dorsal fin. It can grow to 2 m high.

Male sperm whales can be over twice the size of females.

North Pacific Right whale 17 m

Bowhead whale 18 m

Fin whale 22 m

Blue whale 30 m

Female blue whales are bigger than males.

Grey whale 15 m

The bowhead whale has the largest baleen (hair-like bristles used for feeding) of any cetacean; each one can measure 5 m.

Minke whale 12 m

Humpback whale 14 m

Grey whale

BALEEN WHALES

- Baleen whales are also called Mysticeti.
- There are 14 species.
- They don't have teeth, and feed using special hair-like bristles (baleen) instead.
- Most are really big!
- Females are sometimes larger than males.
- They have two blowholes.

SMALL AND SMART

DOLPHINS AND PORPOISES

Dolphins and porpoises are small toothed whales. They look pretty similar, but dolphins have long, beak-shaped mouths.

Although dolphins have a reputation as kind, caring animals, they are ruthless predators of the sea. Orcas, or killer whales, are members of this family and they are some of the planet's most cunning and savage hunters.

KEY FACTS

- Dolphins have a lump of fatty tissue under the skin of the forehead called a melon.

- Dolphins have lots of cone-shaped teeth in their mouth.

- A dolphin does not have ears on the outside of its head. It only has inner ears, which take sound and turn it into messages for the brain.

On the move

Most dolphins and porpoises are fast swimmers, and some can reach top speeds of more than 55 km/h. Moving quickly takes a lot of energy – and oxygen – so these cetaceans often leap out of the water to breathe as they're swimming. As they 'fly' through the air, the animals can stay out of the jaws of any chasing predators, while getting enough air to help power their getaway.

BIG WORD ALERT

PREDATOR

An animal that hunts other animals to eat.

Dolphins have been badly affected by pollution in the oceans and seas. Poisons, especially the deadly metal mercury, are found in the fish they eat, and are then stored in their body.

Dolphins cannot smell. They lost that sense during evolution, when their nostrils moved to the top of their head and became their blowhole.

The shortest dolphins measure less than 150 cm long.

A harbour porpoise has between 86 and 106 teeth. It uses them to grip onto slippery fish.

Dall's porpoises are the most hunted of all cetaceans in the world. Human hunters have killed more than half a million of them for food in the last 50 years.

SMALL STATS

IN A SPIN

Spinner dolphins love to leap out of the water and spin around and around before splashing back into the sea. Some can spin seven times in a single leap. No one really knows why they do this, but it may help them to get rid of little bugs that burrow into their skin, or it may be to do with communication or play.

Ripley's Believe It or Not!®

This dolphin takes a leap over an unsuspecting surfer in Australia! Photographer Matt Hutton caught the rare sight on camera when he decided to try out surf-photography.

When a dolphin mother swims at top speed her little calf can keep up, but how? The baby swims in its mother's slipstream, a hair's breadth away from her. The slipstream is the area of water close to her body where there is less drag, making it easier for the baby to keep up with her.

The slipstream is created by the mother's body as it moves through the water – helping the baby to swim by her side.

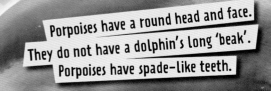

Porpoises have a round head and face. They do not have a dolphin's long 'beak'. Porpoises have spade-like teeth.

HARBOUR PORPOISE

There are six species of porpoise, and one of the smallest is the harbour porpoise. Porpoises usually live in groups of 12 and they hunt fish together, or eat shellfish found on the seabed. Harbour porpoises live mostly in the sea, but have been spotted in rivers!

BIG GULPERS

Meet the leviathans. These are the most massive animals that have ever lived on our planet.

Humpback whale

The hairy bristles in a humpback's mouth (the baleen) probably do more than just trap food like a sieve. Scientists think that the 400 baleen plates in a humpback form a shape-shifting net that changes its shape depending on the speed that water flows through it. That would help a hungry humpback trap even more food.

Baleen whales may be big, but they mostly survive on a diet of very small animals – so they have to eat an enormous quantity of them! They feed using special mouthparts called baleen plates that capture little animals, while allowing water to flow through. Most baleen whales go on long journeys, called migrations, in search of food.

BIG WORD ALERT

LEVIATHAN

A 'sea monster' or any gigantic animal of the sea.

To feed, a whale opens its huge mouth and seawater rushes in.

As water passes through the baleen plates, small animals are trapped on the bristles.

Baleen whales have a big tongue, which they use to swallow food, and push water out of their mouth.

The baleen bristles hang down from the roof of a whale's mouth in 'baleen plates'.

Once, all whales had teeth. As baleen whales evolved, they lost their teeth although for some time there were whales that had baleen and teeth.

Scientists find out what whales eat by opening up the stomachs of dead whales that have washed ashore. They can find out even more by examining bits of whale skin.

Baleen whales love to sing, but they probably do not use echolocation (see page 19) to find food.

GIANT GUZZLERS

A Bryde's whale can be identified by three long ridges on its head. It eats about 660 kg of food a day.

Bryde's whale

Bryde's (say: 'Broodah's') whales are large, fast swimmers that live in warm waters throughout the world's oceans, where they are regularly hunted by whaling boats. Bryde's whales usually live alone or in pairs, and eat small fish and crabs as well as plankton.

It's tough being tiny

The small animals and plants that get carried along by the ocean currents are called plankton. Many of them are too small to be seen with the naked eye – and their normal fate is to be eaten by larger animals than themselves.

Southern right whale

Right whales got their name during whaling times, when hunters said they were the 'right' whales to kill. Today, they are the most rare of all marine mammals, but northern right whales are in even greater danger of extinction than southern right whales. Southern right whales eat copepods – animals so tiny that 8,000 of them would fit on a teaspoon!

Baleen is a tough, but slightly bendy substance and it used to be called 'whalebone'. Although it is like bone, baleen is actually more similar to hair and nails.

GENTLE GIANTS

BLUE WHALES

Imagine you are at sea, when the calm blue of the water's gently rippling surface is broken and a supersized, glistening body emerges.

Witnessing a blue whale as it comes up to breathe can be frightening as well as exciting. These creatures are the biggest of all whales – their size alone is breathtaking. It would be easy for a blue whale to tip a boat over. Blue whales are actually the biggest animals on the planet, but despite their size they are peaceful giants.

A blue whale is a baleen whale and, like other baleen whales, the skin of a blue whale's enormous throat is pleated, with lots of folds and grooves. This makes its skin super-stretchy so it can expand when it fills up with water and food.

When a blue whale prepares to dive it does a 'headstand' and its wide tail appears above the water.

Blue whales surface briefly to release a fountain of air and water and take in a big breath through their blowholes.

TWIST IT!

The part of a blue whale's brain that works out the meaning of sounds (the 'acoustic' part) is ten times bigger than ours.

Scientists don't know when blue whales are old enough to give birth, and they don't know where they give birth!

Whipped cream is 30 per cent fat and whale milk is up to 50 per cent fat – that's as thick as toothpaste!

A blue whale mother is the size of a Boeing 737 airplane, and her newborn baby is the size of a fully-grown hippo.

SUPER-SIZED

BLUE WHALE
Weighs 180 tonnes

=

40 ELEPHANTS
Weigh 4.5 tonnes each

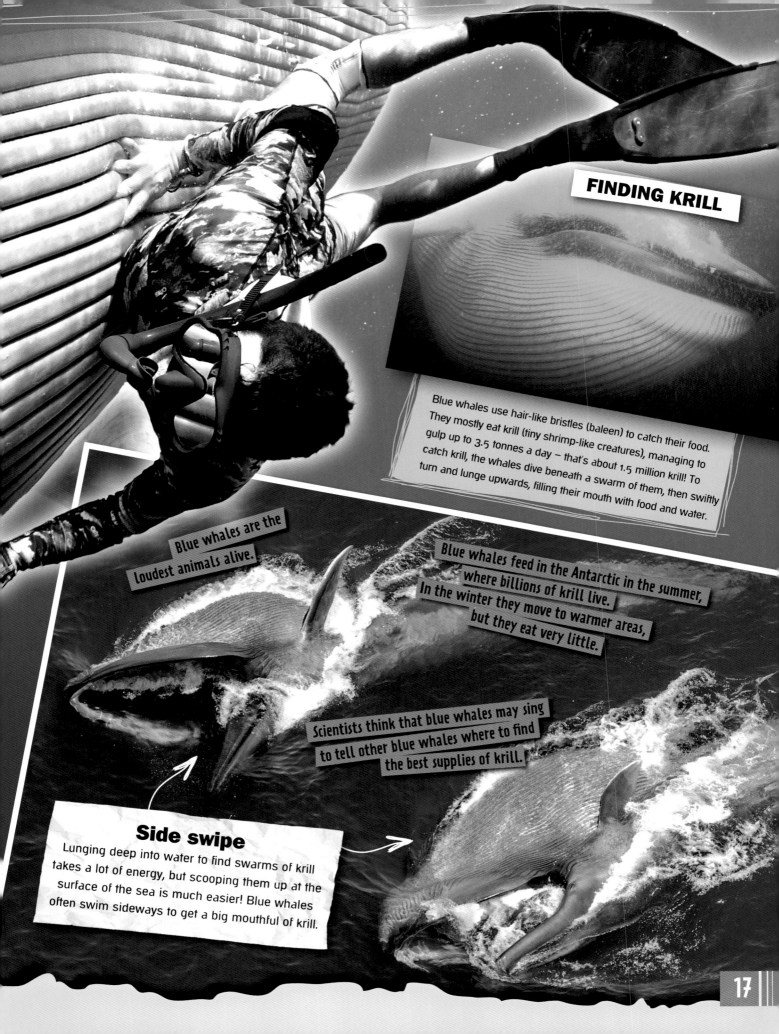

Blue whales use hair-like bristles (baleen) to catch their food. They mostly eat krill (tiny shrimp-like creatures), managing to gulp up to 3.5 tonnes a day – that's about 1.5 million krill! To catch krill, the whales dive beneath a swarm of them, then swiftly turn and lunge upwards, filling their mouth with food and water.

Blue whales are the loudest animals alive.

Blue whales feed in the Antarctic in the summer, where billions of krill live. In the winter they move to warmer areas, but they eat very little.

Scientists think that blue whales may sing to tell other blue whales where to find the best supplies of krill.

Side swipe

Lunging deep into water to find swarms of krill takes a lot of energy, but scooping them up at the surface of the sea is much easier! Blue whales often swim sideways to get a big mouthful of krill.

SOUNDS OF THE SEA

CETACEANS' SENSES

Animals use their senses to find food and to locate other animals. In the deep, dark sea, sound is more important than sight.

Cetaceans (whales, dolphins and porpoises) are masters of the marine environment, with special super senses that help them to find their way – and their prey – in the murky darkness of the ocean. Light does not travel very well under the sea because water absorbs light rays. That is why whales, and many other marine animals, use other senses more than sight to find out what's going on around them.

Sight

Whales and dolphins can see about 9 m ahead when they are underwater. They probably can't see in colour, and don't rely on their sight, although they do have special light-reflecting layers in their eyes that are good at picking up even small amounts of light. Dolphins have better vision than most cetaceans. Their eyes can look in different directions at the same time, which is great for checking for nearby predators!

Small fish swarm together for protection forming a 'bait ball'.

Smell

Scientists have long believed that whales and dolphins do not have a sense of smell, but they have recently discovered that some baleen whales may be able to smell swarms of krill.

Dolphins communicate with each other to take turns herding the bait ball and feeding from it.

Sound

Dolphins don't have ears on the outside of their head. Sound travels through their jaws and other bones in their head. These animals have a superb sense of hearing. This helps them to use their special sense of echolocation (see below). They make sounds – called clicks – that travel through the water and bounce off objects. The sound is 'echoed' back to the animal, allowing them to work out the shape, size and distance of the object.

TWIST IT!

SEA SOUNDS

Bats also use echolocation to hunt prey in the dark.

Dolphins have the most advanced detection system of any animal and by hunting in a group they are extremely skilled at finding and chasing shoals of fast-moving fish.

Submarines use the same system of echolocation as whales and bats to find objects underwater.

Sound waves travel nearly five times faster in sea than in the air.

Ripley explains... Echolocation

All toothed whales use echolocation to locate objects around them. Dolphins produce clicking sounds from their phonic lips just below their blowhole. They use their nasal sacs to move air over the lips to make the sounds. These sounds go out through the front of the dolphin's head. When they hit an object, such as a fish, the sounds bounce back to the dolphin enabling their brain to work out where it is coming from and how big it is.

Nasal sacs
Blowhole
Brain
Returning echo

Taste

Dolphins appear to have a sense of taste, and prefer to eat some fish over others. They also use their sense of taste to find out about other animals. Cetaceans can taste the seawater to detect chemicals (such as wee) that other animals make, so they can get a flavour of what's out there!

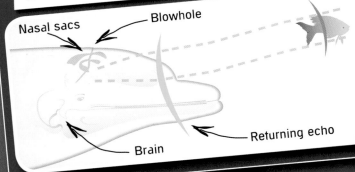

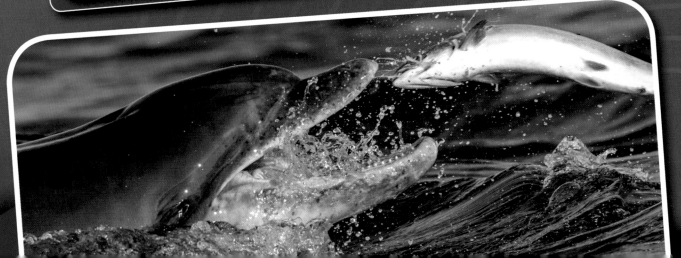

HUNTING WHALES

TOOTHED KILLERS

Ocean hunters are among the most impressive predators on the planet, with their sleek bodies, super speed and killer instincts.

There are few places to hide in the ocean, but finding prey – animals to hunt and eat – is still difficult because the seas are wide, deep and dark. Toothed whales have developed incredible hunting skills to help them find, chase and kill animals.

LEARNING TO KILL

Toothed whales are taught how to find and capture their prey by their mother. Every year, orca mums take their young to Monterey Bay in the United States, where there are many grey whales and their calves. This is where the orcas learn how to kill. The young orcas attack the grey whale calves, while orca mothers watch and help out if needed. It can take the orcas six hours to kill one calf, even when they gang up on it.

A torpedo shaped body is the right shape for moving through water at high speed.

Even though grey whale calves are much larger than adult orcas, orcas use their power and strength to win the fight.

An orca must get a grey whale calf away from its mother before it can attack.

GRAB AND GRIP

Many mammals have different types of teeth, for cutting or grinding. Toothed whales, such as this bottlenose dolphin, however, have just one set of teeth that must last their whole lifetime. The teeth of a toothed whale are all simple and cone-shaped. It is a good shape for grabbing onto slippery fish.

TOP TEAMWORK

These bottlenose dolphins hunt shoals of fish where the water is shallow, working together to force the fish towards the shore. The dolphins even create waves to push the fish out of the water, where they are stranded. The dolphins join the fish on land and eat – this is called strand feeding.

TWIST IT!

Dolphins and other toothed whales are such good hunters that other predators often swim behind them, and feast on their leftovers.

Sometimes hundreds, even thousands, of dolphins gather and travel together. These massive groups are made up of many different families.

Toothed whales can use their echolocation (see page 19) sense to find prey when the water is too dark to see in.

Whales are warm-blooded, like us, and can keep their bodies warm when the water is cold, so they can still swim fast in cold water.

A large group of dolphins is called a herd.

TOUGH TEETH

DEATH BY STEALTH

Toothed whales often hunt in groups, but orcas take the strategy to a whole new level. Scientists know that they 'click' to each other to communicate, but when they begin a hunt orcas switch to silent mode. The seas stay quiet as the orcas come together to co-ordinate and launch their attack, only clicking again to call other orcas to join the feast.

NOWHERE's SAFE

KILLER | WHALES

Orcas (killer whales) are daring, clever predators who attack in the sea and on land.

They are very resourceful, and can even snatch their dinner from beaches! They throw themselves onto the shore in high tide and, unbelievably, manage to grab seal pups. Then, with the catch in their mouth, they use the waves to carry them back out to sea.

Lessons for lunch

If you were a young orca your mum would have to teach you how to get lunch. Here are an orca mother's top tips:

* Whack a group of fish with your strong tail to knock them out.

* Swim under a seal, then use your head to flip it into the air. Have your jaws open wide, and be ready to wolf it down.

* Try a head-butt: simply swim head first at your prey and smash into it with your big strong head.

Killer waves

Orcas sometimes hunt seals that are resting on ice floes. One orca pokes its head above water to look for seals. The other orcas swim at, and under, the floe, creating a wave that tips over the floe and the seal falls into the water. Another orca is waiting to catch the seal.

Ripley's Believe It or Not!®

This lucky gentoo penguin escaped from a pod of hungry orcas off the coast of Antarctica when it jumped onto a boat full of tourists! It then swam away, but returned again later to escape the whales for a second time.

TWIST IT!

Orcas can see just as well out of water as they can underwater. That is useful for an animal that hunts seals, which often rest on ice.

Not all orcas are the same. Scientists think there may be many different types of orca, possibly up to four different species.

A big group of orcas live in the Eastern Pacific Ocean. They are unusual because the males live with their mothers all their lives. We don't know of any other mammals that do this.

In 1978, a pod of orcas was seen chasing a young blue whale. The orcas kept biting the blue whale, which managed to escape but probably died of its injuries soon afterwards.

AWESOME ORCAS

DOLPHIN WORLD

DANCERS OF THE DEEP

Dolphins and porpoises are small toothed whales that live in the sea. There are about 33 types of marine dolphin, six types of porpoise and four types of river dolphin.

Here are some of our favourites...

Finless and friendly

Finless porpoises are small grey cetaceans and are very friendly. They look rather like their cousins, beluga whales. They live near the coast and even swim some distance up rivers. Finless porpoises have a ridge on their back instead of fins, and it's thought that the ridge provides a non-slip surface so calves can grip onto their mum's back and ride along!

Ripley's Believe It or Not!®

Pinky, a rare albino dolphin, was spotted in Lake Calcasieu, Louisiana! It is thought to be the world's only pink bottlenose dolphin.

Timid hunters

Melon-headed whales, also known as little killer whales, are marine dolphins that have a grey, torpedo-shaped body and can change direction at full speed. These shy creatures hunt in the deep seas and usually stay in warm ocean waters, far from the shore.

Friends for life

The shape of a dolphin's face and mouth makes it look as if it's smiling. Scientists can't be sure if a dolphin is happy or not, but these smart animals do often seem to do things just for fun, such as jumping out of the water! Maybe this bottlenose dolphin has found something funny, but the risso dolphin on the right doesn't get the joke!

Show-offs!

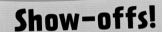

Many dolphins like to leap out of the water as they swim – and Pacific white-sided dolphins are especially graceful when they perform these displays. They often swim alongside boats, and even do somersaults! These are very sociable animals, and sometimes swim in schools of thousands.

Wise workers

Better watch out! When Irrawaddy dolphins pop their head above the surface they often spit water to herd fish! In an astonishing display of intelligence, a group of these animals in Burma work with local fishermen, herding fish into their nets in return for being able to feast on the leftovers. No one taught the dolphins to do this – they worked it out for themselves.

SLEEK SWIMMERS

OCEAN MOTION

Whales are too weighty to live on land, but an ocean is the perfect place for a big-bodied beast to swim with all the grace of a ballet dancer.

If a whale had legs, they would snap under its enormous weight if it tried to walk on land. Even its internal organs, such as the lungs and heart, would be crushed. Water can support heavy animals, making it easier for them to float because it is denser than air. As a result, whales move slowly but gracefully through water.

1st A Dall's porpoise in action!

Speedy swimmer

Dall's porpoises are not just fast, they are agile and super-flexible too. They zigzag, take sharp turns and roll – including a special 'rooster-tailing roll', which is named after the cone of water this movement makes – it looks like a rooster, or cockerel, tail!

Into the sea

Fish swim by moving their tail from side-to-side, but whales move their tail up and down. That's because they are descended from four-legged animals that walked on land, using muscles that moved the spine up and down, not from side-to-side.

Sperm whale

A whale's body is packed with strong muscles to power it forwards.

Speedy cetaceans

The fastest members of the whale family include Dall's porpoises, orcas and sei whales, but none of them comes close to the speed of the world's fastest fish – a sailfish, which has a top speed of 110 km/h. Maybe that's why whales usually target slower swimmers, such as squid!

1st	Dall's porpoise	55 km/h
2nd	Orca	54 km/h
3rd	Sei whale	48 km/h
4th	Fin whale	46 km/h

STREAMLINED SHAPE

Look at this sperm whale's body. It is shaped like a submarine and can move through water easily. This sperm whale is swimming upside down. They sometimes do this when hunting, or just for fun!

TWIST IT!

Humpback whales can leap clear of the water (breach), up to 200 times in a row without tiring.

Blue whales have flippers that are up to 4 m long!

Some whales have blowholes that are big enough for a baby to crawl into!

Big swimmers need big tails. A blue whale's tail is as wide as a football goal – that's about 8 m.

BIG MOVERS

Whale skin is rubbery and smooth (although sperm whales are a little wrinkly), keeping them sleek and streamlined.

Like most whales, the sperm whale has flippers that are small compared to the rest of their body. A whale uses its flippers for changing direction, stopping and balancing.

DEEP DIVERS

Whales breathe at the surface, but they dive down head first to eat. Their tail fins – called flukes – create forward motion, propelling the animal onward and downward in the water.

27

ANCIENT MARINERS

LIFE STORIES

Whales are born big, and growing up takes a long time. These are some of the longest-living animals on Earth.

No one knows for sure exactly how long some of these huge creatures can live for in the wild, because we haven't been watching them for long enough. However, we do know that humpback whales can live for more than 100 years, blue whales can live for up to 100 years, and bowhead whales might reach 200 years of age!

Big babies

Whale and dolphin calves feed on milk made by their mother's body.

Whale babies are called calves. Mothers grow their calves inside their body for a long time. It takes about 16 months for a sperm whale calf to grow before it is born – in comparison humans are pregnant for about nine months. A calf is born underwater, but the mother stays near the surface so she can nudge her baby up to the air to take its first breath.

Mother knows best

Newborn calves stay close to their mother. Some whales live together in families, and all the females help to look after the calves. Sperm whale and grey whale females often feed other females' babies, so the mothers can have a break and go hunting!

Fast learners

Calves, such as this humpback swimming with its mum, copy their mother to learn how to hunt. They stay with their mother for several years, and not all calves leave, even once they are adults.

Great grannies

Grandmothers are also very good at looking after the whole family. They can remember the best places to find food, they lead the family to safe places, and protect the little calves from predators, such as sharks.

A natural end

Many cetaceans live a long life, and die of old age. Others are killed by human and animal hunters. Young cetaceans are preyed on by other whales and sharks.

Ripley's Believe It or Not!®

This very unusual-looking calf, below, is a rare albino humpback whale. It is thought to be the offspring of a famous albino humpback named 'Migaloo', featured on page 43.

FAMILY TIME

A giant bowhead whale caught in 2007 was found to have part of an old harpoon stuck in its side. The harpoon was fired in 1880, so that whale was at least 130 years old.

Sperm whales have been known to attack boats if they think their calves might be in danger.

When a grey whale calf is scared, its mother gently touches it with her fin to reassure it.

Some cetaceans cannot start producing calves until they are in their twenties, but most start their families younger than that.

Female cetaceans usually have just one calf at a time. They can still make milk and feed other calves in the pod even when they are too old to have calves of their own.

Very few people have ever seen a whale give birth in the wild. Even when scientists are lucky enough to see the beginning of a birth, they often move far away, so they don't disturb the mother and her calf.

TWIST IT!

IN DEEP WATER

SPERM WHALES

Sperm whales are the largest toothed whales, and one of the world's biggest predators.

Sperm whales can dive down to around 300 m, where there is no light and few animals can survive. They can stay underwater for nearly two hours, although most dives last less time than this. The sperm whale's deepsea dives are necessary, because its favourite food, the giant squid, is found in the dark ocean depths.

Big head

Sperm whales have a large head that contains a big brain and a strange, waxy substance called spermaceti. This may help a sperm whale to control its buoyancy (how it floats and moves up and down in water). Scientists now think the spermaceti may also help the whale to transmit the clicks and sounds used in echolocation (see page 19).

The whale has small eyes, but it does not need to see well to hunt successfully.

Sperm whales have smooth heads but wrinkly bodies.

The lower jaw is long and narrow with up to 56 teeth. There are no teeth on the top jaw.

The head is huge and box-shaped.

Hungry hunters

Sperm whales eat squid, octopus and fish and they need to eat about 1,000 small squid a day. They are one of the few animals big enough to fight a giant squid – and win.

Underwater battle

Giant squid and sperm whales sometimes get involved in colossal combats. No one has witnessed such a struggle, but models have been built to show what it might look like. The largest squid ever seen to battle with a sperm whale measured 14 m long.

Sperm whales sleep vertically in the water.

Do whales dream?

Sperm whales snatch about 12 minutes of breathless sleep at a time, hanging in the water to enjoy a quick nap. When they sleep, their eyes move backwards and forwards quickly, just like ours do when we dream. Maybe they dream too, but no one knows.

TWIST IT!

Sperm whales can live to 75 years of age and a mother can suckle each calf for up to 12 years!

Sperm whales are the biggest predators that hunt single prey (unlike baleen whales that hunt lots of little animals).

A sperm whale's single blowhole is on the left side of its head rather than the top.

Sperm whales have the largest brain of any creature that has ever lived on Earth.

Male sperm whales are more than twice as heavy as females.

OVER-SIZED

THE PERFECT PLACE

WHALES IN PARADISE

Welcome to paradise! The Gulf of California is a magical place that makes an ideal home for many whales.

It is a narrow strip of water that separates mainland Mexico and a long finger of land, called the Baja Peninsula. The idyllic conditions here create a unique ocean habitat where millions of animals can thrive. Marine biologists – scientists who study life in the oceans – come here to watch whales.

Vaquita porpoise

The vaquita porpoise only lives in the Gulf of California, but it is probably won't even be living there for much longer. It is the world's smallest (measuring just 1.4 m long) and most endangered cetacean. There are only about 200 vaquitas left in the world, which is why we do not have a picture of one here. They are dying out because they get caught in fishing nets.

KEY FACTS

THE GULF OF CALIFORNIA IS HOME TO:

- ☑ 32 species of cetacean (marine mammals)
- ☑ 3,000 species of invertebrates (animals without backbones)
- ☑ over 900 species of fish
- ☑ 170 species of seabird

Short-finned pilot whale

A lovely place to live

The Gulf of California is an area of ocean that is welcoming to many animals because it isn't too hot, and it isn't too cold. In the winter, it is cold at the mouth of the gulf, but stays warm near the top. There are huge tides, and plenty of clean water rushing in. Not many people live on the land nearby, which means not too much pollution gets into the sea and spoils it. All of these things mean that many animals find it a good place to live.

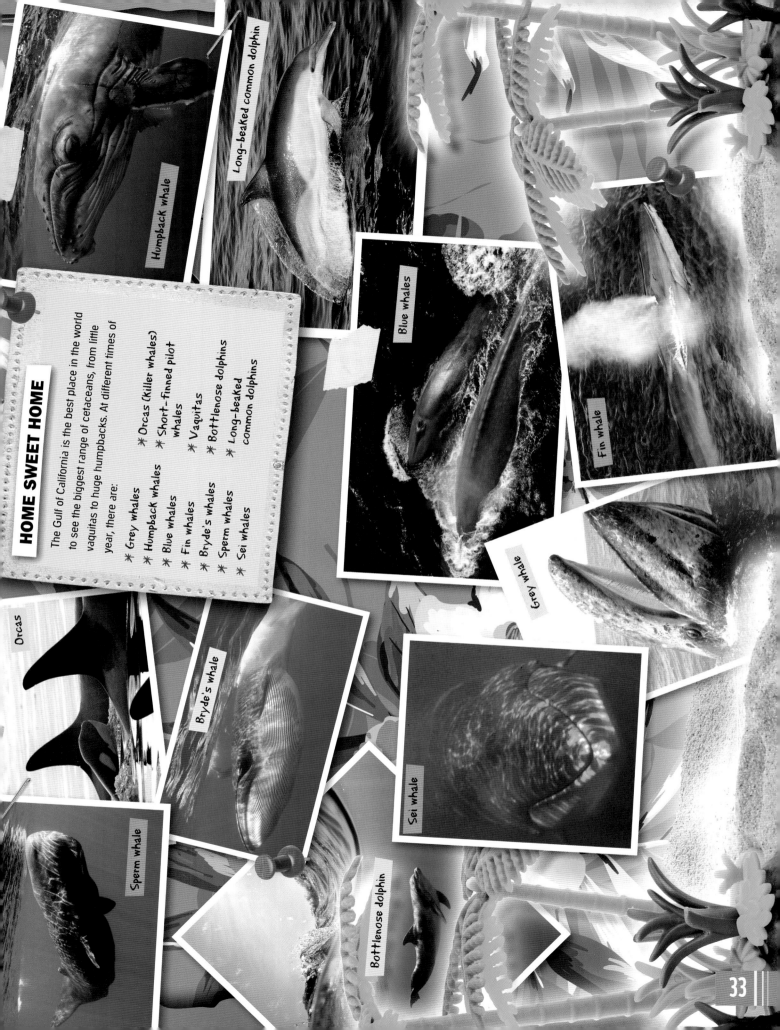

Humpback whale

Long-beaked common dolphin

Blue whales

Fin whale

HOME SWEET HOME

The Gulf of California is the best place in the world to see the biggest range of cetaceans, from little vaquitas to huge humpbacks. At different times of year, there are:

* Grey whales
* Humpback whales
* Blue whales
* Fin whales
* Bryde's whales
* Sperm whales
* Sei whales
* Orcas (killer whales)
* Short-finned pilot whales
* Vaquitas
* Bottlenose dolphins
* Long-beaked common dolphins

Grey whale

Orcas

Bryde's whale

Sperm whale

Sei whale

Bottlenose dolphin

COOL CUSTOMERS

LIFE AT THE COLD POLES

The world's coldest places may look lifeless, but many animals thrive there.

The oceans around the North and South Poles may be chilly, windy, and covered with vast expanses of ice but they are home to many cetaceans. There is enough food here to feed the large populations of dolphins and porpoises, and the biggest whales.

Beluga whales live in groups, or pods, around the Arctic Ocean and 'talk' to each other by making clicking sounds.

The polar regions are extreme places. During the summer, days last for 24 hours, while in winter there is no daylight at all!

The cold waters of the Arctic and Antarctic are home to billions and billions of krill. Seals and penguins eat the krill, and orcas come to feast on the seals and penguins! Baleen whales eat the krill, too.

The white whale

Belugas are small whales that can grow up to 6 m long and live around the Arctic Ocean. Belugas are sometimes called sea canaries because they 'sing' underwater and can make many different sounds. They can also copy the sounds made by other animals. Some divers insist that belugas have copied them when they have called out!

The skin is brown at birth, but gets whiter as the whale ages.

Narwhals mostly swim upside down, on their back. This might be to protect their tusk when they are close to the seabed.

Unicorn whales

Narwhals are the strangest looking whales, with a long spear-like tooth called a tusk. Usually only males have a tusk but sometimes females grow one, and occasionally males grow two. They may use them to fight, or to show off. A good-sized tusk means the narwhal is healthy.

Bowhead whales

The bowhead whale is also known as the Greenland right whale. It holds the record for having the world's biggest mouth, which can be 3 m wide and 6 m deep! It also has a layer of blubber (fat) to help it cope with the Arctic cold that can measure up to 50 cm thick!

No dorsal fin.

A bowhead uses its huge mouth to gulp millions of krill.

White patches around chin.

SMART CETACEANS

BIG THINKERS

All cetaceans, especially dolphins, are smart animals with big brains.

You can teach a dog how to do tricks, but when you show a dolphin how to do a trick, it can change the trick and come up with an even better one! If you play ball with a dolphin it might start to dribble the ball along the seabed, or hold it underwater, then release it suddenly so it shoots up, or blow bubble rings and roll the ball through them.

These artworks represent songs sung by whales and dolphins! Engineer Mark Fischer used special underwater microphones to capture their sounds, even ones we can't hear, and transformed them into images. His work revealed that dolphins have a high level of communication, and even use grammar!

Using tools

Dolphins belong to a special group of animals that can use tools, like humans do. In the 1980s, a female dolphin was seen using a sea sponge on the end of her snout to protect the tip while she dug for food on the seabed. Now, she has taught all the females in her family to use sea sponges!

Talking matters

Being able to communicate, or talk, with each other is a good sign of being smart, and many cetaceans are great talkers. Humpback whales sing to each other, while dolphins call to each other by name. Young calves begin to make their own whistles, which the other dolphins copy and use whenever they want to get that dolphin's attention. Every dolphin has a different whistle-name.

This clever beluga whale in Japan blows bubble rings at the camera!

TWIST IT!

WISE WHALES

Whales speak in dialects — that means their languages are different depending on which area they come from!

Toothed whales hunt and often live in groups, which means they need to be smart and good at communicating with each other.

Male fin whales sing when they feast on krill.

Bottlenose dolphins recognize themselves in mirrors.

Dolphins are able to think, know, and remember in similar ways to humans and apes, but their brains are built in a different way. Scientists think that they can probably recognize numbers, but may not be able to count.

Whale songs have a low frequency, which means they can travel undersea for hundreds — maybe even thousands — of kilometres.

BEYOND THE SEA

RIVER DOLPHINS

Most cetaceans live in salty ocean water, but these little dolphins have found a new home.

Most river dolphins tend to be small, measuring about 2 m long. They live in muddy rivers where the water is murky and it is difficult to see. They have small eyes, but eyesight is not very important to them. They use their sense of echolocation (see page 19) to find prey instead.

Pink river dolphin

The pink, or Amazon, river dolphin is also known as a 'boto'. Most toothed whales have teeth that are all alike, but botos have two different types of teeth. Peg-like teeth catch fish, but molars at the back of their mouth are perfect for crushing crunchy crabs and turtles. Botos sometimes hunt in packs with tucuxis – grey river dolphins – and giant otters.

Habitat: Amazon River and other rivers nearby
Diet: Fish, crabs and turtles
Features: The largest of the river dolphins

ENDANGERED

Most river dolphins share their habitat with people, which is why they are in danger of dying out.

KEY FACTS

River dolphins can grow to a maximum of 2.7 m but most are smaller, and weigh less than 50 kg. They also have:

- ☑ Long, slender beak
- ☑ Bulging forehead
- ☑ Small eyes
- ☑ Neck
- ☑ Broad fins

Pink river dolphins start their life with black skin, but as they age they get pinker.

Irrawaddy dolphins

These small dolphins are hard to see because their freshwater homes are often filthy with pollution. Irrawaddy dolphins are honoured in parts of Cambodia and Laos where they are believed to carry the souls of people who have died. However, they often get trapped in fishing nets.

Habitat: Rivers, coasts and mangrove swamps in Indo-Pacific region

Diet: Fish, squid and crustaceans

Features: Small, rounded head and no 'beak'

VULNERABLE

NOT VULNERABLE

Tucuxi dolphin

Tucuxi (say: too-koo-shi) dolphins can live in the ocean as well as rivers, and they look and behave more like bottlenose dolphins than other river dolphins. Tucuxis often leap out of the water and play in the ripples and waves created by passing boats.

Habitat: Rivers and coasts in South America and eastern Central America

Diet: Mostly fish

Features: A long beak and grey or pinkish skin

ENDANGERED

Blind river dolphins

Ganges river dolphins have terrible eyesight. Their eyes only let in a tiny pinprick of light, but it doesn't matter. Also known as blind river dolphins, these cetaceans use echoes to build up a 'sound picture' of their environment. They also swim on their side, with one flipper touching the riverbed, to help them find food.

Habitat: In and around the Ganges and Brahmaputra Rivers in India and Bangladesh

Diet: Fish, especially carp and catfish

Features: Long fins and large tail fins (flukes)

ENDANGERED

Indus river dolphins

Indus river dolphins are mysterious animals and little is known about how they live and breed. They prefer to swim in deep water rivers, where they hunt large fish. These river dolphins are hunted by local people for food.

Habitat: In and around the Indus River in Pakistan

Diet: Fish, clams and prawns

Features: Live in groups of up to three

MEGA MIGRATIONS

WHALES ON THE MOVE

As grey whales migrate along the North American coastline they stay in shallow water to avoid the attention of hungry orcas.

Grey whales embark on incredible journeys to be in the right place to feed and breed.

Many whales migrate – they go on long journeys. They have big appetites and travel to the places where there is most food. They also migrate to have their babies because they prefer to look after their calves in warm, sheltered waters away from predators. Whales can make these massive migrations because they are big animals and powerful swimmers.

Look at the size of these barnacles!

Big barnacles

A single grey whale may carry more than 450 kg of barnacles. These are crustaceans that glue themselves to the whale's skin and grab food out of the water as the whale swims.

These shell-like barnacles were once attached to a whale. The shells are sharp and act like a suit of armour if the whale is attacked.

ACTUAL SIZE!

JULY–OCTOBER
The whales are at their northern homes in the Bering and Chuckchi seas. They feast on little sea creatures, their calves learn how to eat solid food and they store blubber for their journey south.

Grey whale migration route

FEBRUARY–JUNE
The whales leave their southern home and start the long journey back up north. The young calves stay with their mothers, because they are still dependent on their mother's milk. Most of the whales will be back in the food-filled Arctic waters by June.

BIG WORD ALERT
MIGRATION
A long journey made by an animal in order to mate, have young or find food.

NOVEMBER–JANUARY
There is little food about as the Arctic seas begin to freeze over, so the long journey south to Mexico's warm waters must begin. Whales swim for 24 hours a day. The females are pregnant, and soon start to give birth in the warm seas.

Grey whale mothers can cover 26,000 km in just six months.

TWIST IT!

Hitchhikers

It is common for little animals to cling on to a whale and hitch a ride as it travels through the oceans. Barnacles do not harm the whale, but some animals, such as whale lice, can cause skin damage. Animals that live on another and cause harm are called parasites.

MAKING A MOVE

A grey whale female can cover 145 km in just 24 hours. She can do this for six months – that's more than 26,000 km – and scarcely eats during all that time.

Fin whales travel to the poles in summer to gorge on krill. Fin whales are called greyhounds of the sea because they can swim so fast. They can reach speeds of 46 km/h and cover 290 km in a day.

Whale muscles are packed with a protein that is really good at storing oxygen, so whales can make long, deep dives without taking a breath.

Beluga whales live around the Arctic in the summer, but in the winter the seas freeze over, so they usually migrate south to warmer places.

Female blue whales begin their migration before the males and the oldest whales go the farthest, into the coldest Arctic or Antarctic waters.

No one knows for sure how whales find their way along their migration routes. Scientists think they use both the Sun's position and the Earth's magnetism as a guide.

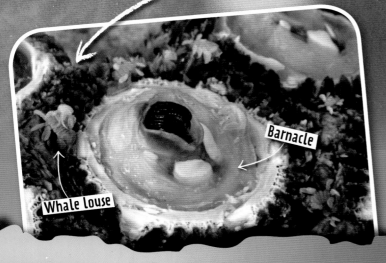

Barnacle

Whale Louse

SONGS OF THE SEA

HUMPBACK WHALES

Humpback whales may be as big as a bus, but they are gentle giants with very impressive acrobatic skills.

Humpbacks are baleen whales (see page 11) and they are famous for their beautiful songs, their long migrations and the amazing way that they catch their food. These energetic whales may be large, but they can flip out of the water, twist in midair and land on their side with a bang.

White markings on long flippers

Throat grooves, or pleats

Blue-black body

TWIST IT!

It takes ten years for a humpback calf to grow to full size.

Humpbacks that live in the Earth's southern oceans eat lots of krill (tiny animals), but those that live in northern places eat much more fish.

Humpback whales have the same special brain cells that humans have to help them live and work in families and groups.

Humpback whales use their flippers to swim, gather fish and stroke their young.

Humpback whales have the world's longest flippers. They can grow to 5 m, which is about one-third of the whale's body length.

GET THE HUMP

Singing sensations

Male humpbacks love to make regular patterns of sound – called singing. They are some of the noisiest animals in the ocean and their 'songs' can last for several hours. When they sing, the males hang in the water, with their head pointing downwards.

Humpback whales

Length: Up to 14 m
Weight: Up to 27 tonnes
Range: Worldwide except the coldest waters
Status: Endangered

Mega migration

Humpback whales gorge on food in the cold oceans near the North and South Poles in the summer, but travel to warm tropical seas to give birth in the winter. During the winter, they eat very little and survive on their stores of fat. Humpbacks in the Indian Ocean may not migrate at all.

Ripley's Believe It or Not!®

Migaloo, as he is known, is thought to be one of the only completely albino whales in the world. Photographer Jenny Dean spotted the white humpback whale while on a whale-watching trip in Australia.

Open wide!

Bubble nets

Humpbacks have developed an amazing way to eat. They swim in circles around a school of fish, breathing out lots of bubbles. The bubbles make a 'curtain of foam' that traps the fish. The whale then swims up through the trap, gulping down large numbers of fish that are caught in the 'bubble net'.

WHALE WATCHING

GETTING TO KNOW YOU

For a long time, people did not understand how special whales and dolphins are. Now we are a much wiser species!

When people discovered that they could use whales for meat, oil (made from whale blubber) and other products they began to hunt some species close to extinction. Most countries of the world now respect a ban on whale hunting, and many populations of whales and dolphins are recovering. Other problems include pollution and over-fishing.

Colossal collision

This blue whale fatally crashed into a ship in the Santa Barbara Channel, California. Blue whales feed in the shipping lane, and as a result there have been dozens of collisions here over the last decade.

STOP PRESS...STOP PRESS...STO

Every day amazing new facts are being discovered about whales and dolphins...

SCIENCE CRACKS THE MYSTERY QUACK

For decades, sailors and submariners have been mystified by strange quacking noises around the Antarctic. The noise – called 'bio-duck' – has now been revealed as the song of Antarctic minke whales.

WONDER WHALE WOWS WORLD WITH NEW RECORD

Extreme divers plunge into the ocean and hold their breath in a dangerous sport called 'free-diving'. The champion 'free-diver' of the world, however, is not a human but a Cuvier's beaked whale. These record-breakers reach depths of nearly 3 km and can stay underwater for up to 137 minutes.

Scientists used satellite tags to follow Cuvier's beaked whales as they dived deeper, and longer, than any other marine mammal.

A WHALE WARNING

Whales and dolphins breed slowly. They often have only one baby in a year, and sometimes one baby every two years.

Cetaceans need clean, quiet water to live in. The oceans are dirtier, noisier and busier places than they used to be, and this has made survival difficult for whales and dolphins around the world.

The world's largest remaining group of blue whales spends summers on the western coast of the United States and Mexico. There are just 3,000 of them left.

About two million whales in total died when whaling was allowed.

Tagging whales

It's not easy to follow whales underwater! The best way for scientists to find out where they go and what they do is to tag them. Each tag is a mini-computer that sends messages about a whale's movements to a satellite in space. The tag also measures the water temperature, pressure, amount of salt in it and sunlight. The information gathered by doing this helps scientists to make new discoveries about these amazing creatures.

PLAY TIME FOR TALKING DOLPHINS

Dolphin researchers have even taught some of their finned friends to whistle out sounds such as 'scarf' and 'rope' when they want to play with these objects!

WHISTLING DOLPHINS GIVE EACH OTHER NAMES

Scientists have discovered that when a dolphin wants to get hold of one of its pals it grabs its attention by calling out its name! That's right, a group of dolphins uses a different whistle to call each member of the family.

RESS...STOP PRESS...STOP PRESS

A brighter future

Today, people want to learn more about these big, beautiful beasts. Scientists and wildlife-lovers sail across the ocean to watch and photograph them, rather than hunt them.

INDEX

Bold numbers refer to main entries; numbers in *italic* refer to illustrations

ACKNOWLEDGEMENTS

COVER (sp) © Chua Han Hsiung - shutterstock.com, (t) © Natali Glado - shutterstock.com; **2** © Shane Gross - shutterstock.com; **3** (t) Rex/Masa Ushioda/SplashdownDirect, (b) © anyamuse - shutterstock.com; **4** © Monika Wieland - shutterstock.com; **6** © David Herraez Calzada - shutterstock.com; **7** (t) © Karoline Cullen - shutterstock.com, (b) Rex/Masa Ushioda/SplashdownDirect; **8–9** Leonardo Meschini; **10** (t/l) Jurgen & Christine Sohns/FLPA, (b/l) © Thumbelina - shutterstock.com, (t/r, b/r) © laschi - shutterstock.com, (c/l) © dkvektor - shutterstock.com, (t/c) © Ilya Akinshin - shutterstock.com; **11** (t/c/l, t/l, b/l) © Thumbelina - shutterstock.com, (t/c/r, c/l) © Nebojsa Kontic - shutterstock.com, (b/c, t/r) © laschi - shutterstock.com, (b/r) © Biosphoto, Christopher Swann/Biosphoto/FLPA; **12** (sp) © Juniors Tierbildarchiv/Photoshot, (t) © anyamuse - shutterstock.com; **13** (t) Flip Nicklin/Minden Pictures/FLPA, (c/r) Caters News Agency Ltd., (c/l) Konrad Wothe/Minden Pictures/FLPA, (b) Solvin Zankl/Visuals Unlimited, Inc. /Science Photo Library; **14** Jill M Perry; **15** (t) © Doc White/seapics.com, (b) Hiroya Minakuchi/Minden Pictures/FLPA; **16** (b/l) © aleksander1 - fotolia.com, (b/r) © a_elmo - fotolia.com; **16–17** (dp) Matthew Stewart Coutts; **17** (t) © Doug Perrine/seapics.com, (b) © Doc White/naturepl.com; **18–19** (bgd) Alexander Safonov/Getty Images; **19** (t) © Aflo/naturepl.com, (c) Dynamo Design, (b) Rex/FLPA/Dickie Duckett; **20** Brandon Cole; **21** (t) © Pedro Narra/naturepl.com, (c) © Todd Pusser/naturepl.com, (b) FLPA/Rex; **22** Sylvain Cordier/Biosphoto/FLPA; **23** (t) Alain Bidart/Biosphoto/FLPA, (b) R. Roscoe (photovolcanica.com); **24** (t) © Masa Ushioda/seapics.com, (c) Caters News Agency Ltd., (b) © Doug Perrine/naturepl.com; **25** (t) © A. L. Stanzani/ardea.com, (c) © Brandon Cole/naturepl.com, (b) EPA/Barbara Walton; **26** (t) Minden Pictures/Getty Images; **26–27** (b) © Brandon Cole/naturepl.com; **27** (r) © Dan Bach Kristensen - shutterstock.com; **28** (t/r) © Franco Banfi/naturepl.com; **28–29** (dp) © Amos Nachoum/seapics.com; **29** (b/r) Sam Ruttyn/Newspix/Rex; **30** (t) © Nature Production/naturepl.com; **30–31** (dp) © Nature Production/naturepl.com; **31** (t/r) © Susan Dabritz/seapics.com; **32** (c) Sam South, (b) © Rainer Lesniewski - shutterstock.com; **32–33** (bgd) © SalomeNJ - shutterstock.com; **33** (t/c) © Sergey Uryadnikov - shutterstock.com, (t/l) © Joost van Uffelen - shutterstock.com, (t/r) © Juan Gracia - shutterstock.com, (c) © Doug Perrine/naturepl.com, (c/l) © Monika Wieland - shutterstock.com, (c/r) Hiroya Minakuchi/Minden Pictures/FLPA, (b/c) © Willyam Bradberry - shutterstock.com, (b/l) © Shane Gross - shutterstock.com, (b/r) Mammal Fund Earthviews/FLPA, (b/c/r) © James Michael Dorsey - shutterstock.com; **34** (sp) © Doug Allan/naturepl.com; **35** (t) © Franco Banfi/naturepl.com, (c) © Doc White/ardea.com, (b) © Martha Holmes/naturepl.com; **36** (t, b/r) Aguasonic Acoustics/Science Photo Library, (b/l) © Hugh Pearson/naturepl.com; **37** (t) © KateChris - shutterstock.com, (b) Rex/KPA/Zuma; **38** Kevin Schafer/Minden Pictures/FLPA; **39** (t) © Roland Seitre/naturepl.com, (b) © Andrea Florence/ardea.com; **40** (c) © Todd Pusser/naturepl.com, (b) © Michael S. Nolan/seapics.com; **40–41** (dp) Rex/Gerard Lacz; **41** (t) Dynamo Design, (b) Frans Lanting/FLPA; **42** © Biosphoto, Christopher Swann/Biosphoto/FLPA; **43** (t) Jenny Dean/Rex Features, (b) © Brandon Cole/naturepl.com; **44** (t) Flip Nicklin/Minden Pictures/FLPA, (b/l) Norbert Wu/Minden Pictures/FLPA, (b/r) © Todd Pusser/naturepl.com; **45** (t) Flip Nicklin/Minden Pictures/FLPA, (b) Rex/SplashdownDirect/Michael Nolan

Key: t = top, b = bottom, c = centre, l = left, r = right, sp = single page, dp = double page, bgd = background

All other photos are from Ripley's Entertainment Inc. All other artwork by Dynamo Design Ltd.

Every attempt has been made to acknowledge correctly and contact copyright holders and we apologise in advance for any unintentional errors or omissions, which will be corrected in future editions.